W...

YOUR SPIRITUAL BATTLES

TONY EVANS

HARVEST HOUSE PUBLISHERS
EUGENE, OREGON

Cover by Bryce Williamson

Cover photos © Nacho Mena, chingraph / Getty Images

Winning Your Spiritual Battles
Taken from *Victory in Spiritual Warfare*
Copyright © 2011 by Tony Evans
Published by Harvest House Publishers
Eugene, Oregon 97408
www.harvesthousepublishers.com

ISBN 978-0-7369-7942-9 (pbk)
ISBN 978-0-7369-7943-6 (eBook)

Library of Congress Cataloging-in-Publication Data is on file at the Library of Congress, Washington, DC

Printed in the United States of America

21 22 23 24 25 26 27/ BP-CD / 10 9 8 7 6

CONTENTS

Acknowledgments

I want to thank my friends at Harvest House Publishers for their long-standing partnership in bringing my thoughts, study, and words to print. I particularly want to thank Bob Hawkins for his friendship over the years, as well as his pursuit of excellence in leading his company. I also want to publicly thank Terry Glaspey, Nick Harrison, and Gene Skinner for their help in the editorial process. In addition, my appreciation goes out to Heather Hair for her skills and insights in collaboration on this manuscript.

1

THE NATURE
OF THE BATTLE

In an art gallery in Europe hangs a painting titled *Checkmate*. On one side of a chessboard sits the devil, full of laughter. His hand is poised, ready to make his next move. On the other side of the chessboard sits a shaking, frightened young man. Sweat covers his forehead, dripping down and mixing with a solitary tear on his cheek. The game is obviously drawing to a close, and the winner appears to have already been decided.

One day, a chess champion from a far off country visited the gallery. Naturally, the painting caught his attention, inviting him to examine it for a very long time. In fact, while others had moved on throughout the gallery, the chess champion remained fixated on the game and especially on the devil, who sat eagerly waiting for his next turn, in which he planned to steal this man's soul.

Minutes turned into hours as the chess champion studied the board from every possible angle. The sweat on the young man's forehead urged him to continue.

Finally, as the gallery was about to close, the chess champion found the proprietor of the gallery and asked him, "Sir, would you happen to have a chessboard here?"

After looking around in several of the offices, he located a chessboard and brought it to the man. The chess champion laid the board out at the base of the painting precisely as it was in the painting. He made a move and then countered that move in the only way that the devil could to avoid checkmate. He then made another move, and countered it again knowing that the devil would have to defend himself in his next move as well. The chess champion did this several more times, putting the devil on the defensive each and every time. Eventually, a loud yell was heard throughout the gallery as the chess champion cried out in relief, "I did it! I did it! I did it!"

Turning to the painting, the chess champion lowered his voice and said, "Young man, your enemy miscalculated a very important move. I uncovered it, and as a result, you don't have to lose! You win!"

This chess champion had discovered a way not only for the young man to escape but also to checkmate the devil himself.

Friend, if you have picked up this book, the chances are that you may have felt like the man in the painting. Fear or anxiety has crept up on you as you imagine the devil preparing to make the final move in your personal life, marriage, home, health, career, finances, or any number of other arenas. Satan's confident laughter and swift moves have tricked you into believing that he is running the show and calling the shots. He has been toying with your emotions as if you were a puppet on a string.

But as we journey through this study together, I encourage you to wipe the sweat from your forehead and dry the tears from your eyes. You can do this because you have a Champion who knows how to guide your every move. In fact, this Champion has already made the final move on the devil, securing your victory forever. If you will simply play out the remainder of the game according to His directions and underneath the overarching rule of His kingdom agenda, you will claim your victory. That is guaranteed.

The great thing is that you don't have to earn your victory, nor do you have to figure it out for yourself. God has already given you everything you need in order to make your next move on your path to triumph. As we begin, I want you to realize this key principle: You are not fighting *for* victory—you are fighting *from* victory. This battle has already been won!

The History of the Battle

To grasp the truth behind this principle, you first need to understand the history of the battle. It all began when God made the first move by creating the angels. Lucifer, the anointed angel, responded negatively to that move by rebelling against God and taking one-third of the angels with him in that rebellion. God countered that move by creating man, in His own image, a little lower than the angels. Satan rebelled against that move by enticing Adam and Eve to sin, thus turning earth over to his control.

God then countered Satan's move by providing a redemptive covering for Adam and Eve so they could return back to fellowship with God. Satan made his next move by inciting Cain to kill Abel in order to cut off the godly line.

But God responded to Satan's move through the birth of Seth, making a way for men to begin calling on the name of the Lord again. Satan countered that move by luring Nimrod at the Tower of Babel into thinking he could make himself and his people as high as the heavens.

For God's next move, He turned His gaze onto a man named Abraham, calling out a nation through him to be holy and set apart. Satan, however, countered that move by trapping this nation in Egypt under Pharaoh's rule. But then God grabbed Moses in Midian and placed him in position to knock Pharaoh out of the equation altogether.

Throughout the remainder of the Old Testament, the game went on like this—move, countermove, move, countermove. By the end of the Old Testament, we have reached a time of four hundred years where no move is recorded by either side as both sit staring at the board in silence.

But when the New Testament opens up, we see God reach for a special piece—His own son, Jesus Christ—and move Him into a new location, from heaven to earth. Satan attempts to counter God's move by tempting Jesus in the wilderness. Jesus overcomes his move through using the Word of God. So Satan then tries what he thinks is going to be his final move of checkmate by orchestrating the crucifixion of Jesus Christ. But Satan miscalculated something very important because he didn't realize that death on the cross was not a checkmate move. In fact, it was just a setup for the final move that God would make to checkmate Satan by raising Jesus from the dead.

The accomplishment of the cross, through the resurrection of Christ, was God's final move and offered each one of us victory over an enemy who is seeking to intimidate, deceive, and destroy us. The ultimate winner of this game has been decided. Victory has been secured. While you and I are on earth and still in play, we need to live in light of the truth of the victory gained through that final move—the resurrection of Jesus Christ. Because of that decisive move by God, Satan no longer has authority over you to defeat you. His only means to overcome you is to deceive you—to make you believe that the winner of the battle is yet undecided.

How the Spiritual Impacts the Physical

By illustrating spiritual warfare though a simple game of chess, I don't mean to minimize the severity of the battle nor the enormous depth of pain and number of casualties that have resulted from it. It *is* a battle. We are in a war. In fact, the war we are in is like no other war that any of us have ever known or heard about or could even conceive. If I were to ask you to think of the absolute worst war in human history, it would pale in comparison to the spiritual battle waging all around us.

This war is different from all other wars not only because of its sheer magnitude and scope but also because this war is fought in a place we have never seen. Spiritual warfare is *the cosmic conflict waged in the invisible, spiritual realm but simultaneously fleshed out in the visible, physical realm.* To put it another way, the *root* of the war is something you cannot see, but the *effects* of the war are clearly seen and felt. This is because everything physical is either influenced or caused by something spiritual.

Behind every physical disturbance, setback, ailment, or issue we face lies a spiritual root. Unless we first identify and deal with the root spiritual cause, our attempts to fix the physical problem will provide only temporary relief at best. In other words, everything that your five senses experience physically is first generated by something that your five senses cannot detect.

In light of this truth, you and I need to engage a sixth

sense—a spiritual sense—when doing battle in this war. We must employ that which goes beyond physiology and address the spiritual root before we can truly fix the physical fruit. Here is the key to experiencing and living out on earth the victory that God has already secured in heaven: to learn how to intentionally and effectively do battle in the spiritual realm.

Satan often tries to prevent you from taking the spiritual realm seriously. If he can divert your attention away from the spiritual realm, he can keep you away from the only place where your victory is found. If he can distract you with people or things you can see, taste, touch, hear, or smell, he can keep you from living a life of victory.

The Location of the Battle

This battle is so important and its spoils so costly, it is essential that we start at the beginning and lay a solid foundation for our strategy. The first thing you need to know is where this battle takes place. Paul gives us the answer in the sixth chapter of Ephesians, which is the passage we will be using as the basis for our study throughout this book.

> Finally, be strong in the Lord and in the strength of His might. Put on the full armor of God, so that you will be able to stand firm against the schemes of the devil. For our

struggle is not against flesh and blood, but against the rulers, against the powers, against the world forces of this darkness, against the spiritual forces of wickedness *in the heavenly places* (Ephesians 6:10-12).

Paul tells us that our battle is not against flesh and blood. Our battle is not against our neighbor, spouse, coworker, child, or even our own propensities or weaknesses in our flesh. People are simply conduits of the spiritual battle taking place in another realm. Our battle, according to the Word of God, is against the rulers, powers, and world forces of wickedness located in heavenly places. "Heavenly places" simply means in the spiritual realm.

Here's a second principle I want you to take hold of: Whatever has gone on, is going on, or will go on in your visible, physical world is rooted in the invisible, spiritual realm. If you do not know how to navigate in the spiritual realm, you cannot hope to truly overcome in the physical realm.

This highlights a problem we often run into. We usually try to fix things in the physical realm by using methods of this world even though this world is not where our problems originate. We are like a police officer in his living room shooting his TV because he sees a criminal on a reality show pulling a gun. If the officer shoots at the television, he will have merely added to the mess that's going on. He might feel better for a moment because he did something, but in the end, nothing has been solved. In fact, things have only gotten worse.

Our battles originate in the spiritual realm—the heavenly places—so the only way to fight them is with weapons that work in that realm.

Heavenly Places

Paul uses the phrase "heavenly places" a number of times in the book of Ephesians, letting us know both the scope and occupants of the location. His first reference to this realm comes in chapter 1, verse 3: "Blessed be the God and Father of our Lord Jesus Christ, who has blessed us with *every spiritual blessing* in the heavenly places in Christ."

We learn from this verse that everything God is ever going to do for us, He has already done. Every spiritual blessing is already located in this unseen realm. Every promise God has ever made and plans to fulfill on your behalf, every gift you will ever receive, and every hope that will ever be satisfied has already been deposited in your account in the spiritual realm. God has "blessed us with *every* spiritual blessing in the heavenly places in Christ." Your blessings and victory are already located there with your name written on them, waiting for you to grab them, use them, and walk in them.

Many believers live defeated lives simply because they are unaware of this truth. Yet Paul makes it clear in this passage that we have already been blessed with *every* spiritual blessing in the spiritual realm.

In spiritual warfare, Satan tries to deceive you into believing that God is holding out on you and that it is up to you to get God to give you both blessings and victory. Satan wants you to think that if you pray more, give more, serve more, sin less, do better, or worship more, maybe God will give you more. This shifts the focus off of God and what He has already done in the spiritual realm and puts the focus on you and what you need to do in the physical realm. Doing those things in the physical realm is good and beneficial for spiritual growth and cultivating intimacy with God and others, but those things are not the keys to accessing what God already has for you in the spiritual realm.

The way to access the power of your blessings is through a biblical understanding and application of grace through faith. In grace, God has made every believer complete in Jesus Christ. Religious "works" that we do in an effort to get something from God actually nullify grace (Galatians 5:1-4) because grace and works can never be mixed (Romans 11:6). Grace is the point of access to God.

The way we enter this point of access is through faith. Faith is acting as if God is telling the truth. It is acting as if something is true even when it doesn't *appear* to be true in order that it might *be shown to be* true simply because God *said* it's true. The job of faith is to discover what the spiritual blessings in the heavenly places already are, ask God for them, and make life choices in light of that reality. We will look more deeply at grace and faith a little later.

The Occupants

So far we have seen that you are not fighting *for* victory—you are fighting *from* a position of victory. We have also seen that whatever has gone on, is going on, or will go on in your physical world is rooted in the spiritual realm. And every spiritual blessing is located in this spiritual realm. Paul tells us more about the spiritual realm when he writes, "These are in accordance with the working of the strength of His might which He brought about in Christ, when He raised Him from the dead and *seated Him* at His right hand in the heavenly places" (Ephesians 1:19-20).

Paul has already told us that our blessings are waiting for us to access them in heavenly places, and he now tells us that the One who is in charge, Jesus Christ, is seated in these same heavenly places. That means that if you want to get to the One who is in charge—Jesus—you will need to approach Him where He is—in the spiritual realm, the heavenly places. In the next chapter of Ephesians, Paul gives us more details about this.

> But God, being rich in mercy, because of His
> great love with which He loved us, even when
> we were dead in our transgressions, made us
> alive together with Christ (by grace you have
> been saved), and raised us up with Him, and
> *seated us with Him* in the heavenly places in
> Christ Jesus (Ephesians 2:4-6).

We've seen that our blessings are located in heavenly places and that Jesus Christ is seated in heavenly places. Now we learn that *we ourselves* are seated with Jesus in these same heavenly places. Right this very minute, you and I are spiritually seated with Christ in the spiritual realm.

This is an important truth to remember. If you are focusing only on where you are sitting right now physically, you are not viewing your location as being in the same place as where the solutions to your problems actually exist. Where you are physically is not the only place you are located. You are equally located in another realm. Paul tells us that at the moment you trusted in Christ for your salvation, you were transported to another realm. Even though your physical body is here on earth, your spirit—the part of you that has been designed with the capacity to control your physical body—is operating in another location.

Paul tells us more about this other location in the next chapter of Ephesians.

> To me, the very least of all saints, this grace was given, to preach to the Gentiles the unfathomable riches of Christ, and to bring to light what is the administration of the mystery which for ages has been hidden in God who created all things; so that the manifold wisdom of God might now be made known through the church *to the rulers and the authorities* in the heavenly places (Ephesians 3:8-10).

Not only are your spiritual blessings, Jesus Christ, and you yourself located in the spiritual realm at this point in time, the angels (rulers and authorities) are also operating in the spiritual realm. Why is this important to know? Because it is better to have an angel battling a demon than to battle a demon yourself in your flesh. If you are facing a demonic problem, you need an angelic solution.

The Bible calls God "the Lord of hosts." That name refers to His military charge over an angelic corps whose job is to go up against any demonic actions that are attacking you. You may be physically strong, you may lift weights, and you might be powerful in your body, but trust me—you are no competition for a demon. In order to call on angelic help, you need to have a heavenly mindset because angels do battle in heavenly places.

What is critical to note in our look at angels is that

every Christian has at least one angel who has been assigned to operate on his or her behalf in the spiritual realm. We read in Hebrews 1:14 (NIV), "Are not all angels ministering spirits sent to serve those who will inherit salvation?" You have someone who knows and understands the spiritual realm better than you and whose job is to function in that realm in a way that benefits you. That is a potent truth.

Yet while every Christian has an angel whose task is to minister to him or her from heavenly places, every Christian also has demonic opposition whose goal is to make all hell break loose in his or her life. We saw in our previous look at Ephesians 6:12 that "the spiritual forces of wickedness" (demons) are also located "in the heavenly places."

So Paul tells the church at Ephesus that our blessings are in the heavenly places, Jesus is in the heavenly places, we are in the heavenly places, angels are in the heavenly places, and the demonic realm is in the heavenly places. With so much going on in the heavenly places, it only makes sense that we should learn and apply as much as we can on how to function and operate effectively in heavenly places. After all, we are in a war where ground zero is located in the heavenly places.

The physical world simply manifests what is already happening in the spiritual realm. If you are unaware of the reality of the spiritual realm, you will be unaware of how that realm operates, causing you to be unprepared and ill equipped to live out your victory in your physical life.

I recently had the chance to see the blockbuster film *Inception,* which illustrated a similar truth cinematically. In the film, the main characters had discovered a way to enter into another realm—the realm of dreams. The dreams appeared to be as vivid and as authentic as the real world they were currently sleeping in, but the dream realm was not real.

Because the dream appeared to be real to all of their five senses, each character had to choose an item that would let them know whether they were in a dream or in reality. Without the item, the person in the dream might begin to believe that the dream was reality, and he or she might stay there—operating by the laws of reality within the realm of a dream.

The main character's item was a spinning top. If his top kept spinning endlessly, that meant he was in a dream. The knowledge that he was in a dream then affected the way he functioned within the dream. Essentially, he could take more risks and live differently in the dream because he knew that at any time, he could simply wake back up in reality.

I'm not suggesting that the physical world we live in is a dream or that physical realities do not carry with them both physical and spiritual consequences. But I want us to realize that our ultimate reality is taking place in the heavenly places—in the spiritual realm. Conversations, decisions, battles, and the like that occur in the spiritual realm unilaterally impact what takes place in our physical lives. Unless we realize that truth, we will continue to look for physical solutions to solve spiritual problems manifesting themselves in our physical lives.

Thankfully, God has given us an item to use—a guide—that we are to look at in order to remind us of our true spiritual location, and that is His Word. When we read God's Word, we are reminded that all spiritual warfare, as well as our solutions for that warfare, are located in the spiritual realm. This world is not our home. As believers we are citizens of and seated in the heavenly realm.

Physical solutions cannot fix physical problems that originate in the spiritual realm. So rather than spending all of our time, money, effort, strength, mental energy, conversations, and anything else we can come up with to help us fare better in the physical world, we ought to first be learning and applying spiritual warfare practices and techniques, so we can defeat our enemy and access our blessings in the spiritual realm.

The demonic realm doesn't want you to know that. The demonic realm wants you to continue to live and do battle in the world of your five senses so that you will try to fix your situation with the limited weapons associated with your five senses. What ends up happening, though, is that a lot of time, money, and energy gets wasted trying to do away with bad fruit while not addressing the spiritual root. But remember this principle: *If all you see is what you see, you will never see all that there is to be seen.*

Since the invisible realm affects the visible realm, if you want to fix something in the physical realm, you must first address the invisible and spiritual root behind it. A failure to address the invisible, spiritual cause simply leads to a failure to experience a long-term and complete visible, physical cure.

Studying Satan's Game

Paul tells us that we wrestle not against flesh and blood, but against the powers and rulers in the spiritual realm. These powers seek to rob you of all that God has stored up for you in the heavenly places. But Paul encourages each of us to wrestle in a unique way—by standing firm against the enemy's schemes and strategies.

One way to stand firm is to learn what those strategies are. Beings in the demonic realm don't want you to know their methodology. They don't want you to figure out their approach. They want you to continue to picture them with horns and a pitchfork and wearing a red jumpsuit. If you continue to think of demonic beings in that way, you will not take them seriously. Nor will you battle them effectively.

Everyone who knows me knows I love football. When I was young, I played football every week. A leg injury sidelined me early on from pursuing the sport, but my passion for the game has never diminished.

Football is the consummate male sport. Well-trained athletes battle it out with precision moves and power-packed plays filling every second of 60 minutes with elevated levels of testosterone similar to those of the gladiators in previous centuries.

One of the highlights of my ministry has been getting to serve on the frontlines of these battles as a chaplain not only in football but also in basketball. I've been the chaplain for the NBA's Dallas Mavericks for more than 30 years. I also served as chaplain for the NFL's Dallas Cowboys during the height of Coach Tom Landry's era, and I currently teach at the Dallas Cowboys' Bible study as well as provide personal counseling for any of the players who need it.

Football is a great life coach. It teaches us the value of self-discipline, determination, and hard work. It also teaches us how to not only outplay our opponents but also outsmart them.

Before an upcoming game, players watch what is called game film. Watching game film includes viewing clips from the upcoming opponent's previous games. The purpose of watching the film is to identify the opponent's weaknesses. Once those weaknesses are identified, a plan is put together on how to best go about exploiting those weaknesses.

If you are a football player, watching film is a good thing to do prior to a game because it gives you an edge you would not normally have over your opponent. The only problem is that your opponent also has film of your games and is studying it to exploit your weaknesses.

In the spiritual war, our opponent, the devil—along with his team of demons—has had thousands of years watching humanity's film. He's an expert on exploiting personality weaknesses, traumas, racial and gender divisions, our flesh and its desires, and many other areas of our human nature. And the demonic realm has been watching your own game film and mine since our conception.

Satan and his demons know what happened to you when you were a child that messed up your thinking, lowered your self-esteem, or led to sin patterns that now seem unbreakable in your life. They know about the issues and abuse (either to you or from you) that operate within your physical world. They know what frustrates you or wears you down, thus giving them an opportunity to move in on you. And they have one purpose for watching your film and gathering this knowledge: to exploit your weaknesses to their advantage in order to defeat you.

This may sound bleak, but the good news is that we also have access to game film. Not only that, but we have a Coach who knows our opponent's weaknesses, and He has told us what those weaknesses are in His Word. He has given us a step-by-step summary of the game film—the Bible. In it, we discover everything we need to know in order to experience victory in this spiritual battle.

Any NFL team that takes to the field on any given Sunday that has not done its homework by first studying its opponent is setting itself up for defeat. In fact, any player who would run out into the game unprepared like that would not find himself being a player for much longer.

The same is true in the Christian life. God has given each of us everything we need to defeat our enemy, but it is up to us to watch the film and to play according to His rules and strategies. Our enemy is a crafty opponent, and unless we do battle against him correctly, he will outwit us. After all, he has our game film. He knows just what button to push to get you to go somewhere you never thought you would go—both in your emotions and your actions. Satan has your game film. It's time for you to study his.

The story is told about a farmer who was perpetually having his melons stolen by thieves. He had to come up with something to do about this theft, or he was going to end up losing a large amount of his profits. So the farmer came up with a brilliant idea. He decided to post a sign on his farm that read, "One of these melons is poisonous."

The next day, the farmer went out to view his melons, and he discovered what he thought would be the case all along—none of his melons had been stolen. Satisfied that he had outsmarted the thieves, the farmer went about the rest of his day smugly filled with gratification. However, the following day, when the farmer went back to work in his field, he saw that the word "One" had been scratched out on his sign. Scribbled next to it was the word "Two." The sign now read, "Two of these melons are poisonous." The farmer lost his entire crop because he didn't know which other melon had been poisoned.

That story is a lot like dealing with the devil. No matter what you or I come up with, Satan is going to try to come up with something better. No matter what New Year's resolution or positive-thinking ten-step plan you or I make, Satan is going to try to knock us off course by the time we take step number one. The only way to live in the victory that has been secured for us in spiritual warfare is to study Satan's game film, learn his strategies and weaknesses, and stand firm in God's strength and according to God's prescribed plays in the heavenly realm.

We cannot outwit or outsmart the father of lies and master of deception. To try to do so on our own would be foolish. If winning this spiritual chess game were left up to us, we would be sweating and crying like the young man in the painting I mentioned at the beginning of the chapter. In fact, many of us take it upon ourselves to battle this war in our own strength and with our own wisdom, so we *are* sweating and crying more than we ought.

However, we have a Champion who has already

studied every move on the game board. He knows what we need to do to finish this game well. It's time to put God's strategies for victory in spiritual warfare into practice and make the devil and his demons the ones who sweat and cry instead.

What do you say? Are you ready to view some game film? Let's take a look and advance in victory.

2

THE OPPOSITION
IN THE BATTLE

The apostle Paul shows us a clip of Satan's game plan when he writes in a passage we referenced in chapter 1: "Finally, be strong in the Lord and in the strength of His might. Put on the full armor of God, so that you will be able to stand firm against the *schemes* of the devil" (Ephesians 6:10-11). The word "schemes" simply means "deceptive strategies." Satan's overarching strategy, which he carries out in many ways, is to deceive. He is the ultimate magician, operating not only with smoke and mirrors but also by sleight of hand.

In fact, we read in Genesis chapter 3 that when Adam and Eve were in the garden, Satan came to them in the form of a snake. The snake was the most deceptive of all the animals that God had created (verse 1).

The reason Satan took on the form of a snake is because he and his demons operate best when there is a physical presence through which to work. Remember this principle: While spiritual warfare is being waged in heavenly places, our enemy is very skilled at locating available vehicles in the physical realm through which to influence, manipulate, and deceive.

Satan even comes to you in a form that you would not suspect. Paul tells us in 2 Corinthians 11:14, "Satan disguises himself as an angel of light." This adds another dimension to the problems we face and fight in the spiritual realm because our problems do not exist only in the invisible spiritual realm; they also exist in the often unsuspecting vehicle Satan uses to get to you in the physical realm, which includes you—your mind, will, emotions, and body.

Satan's Agenda

Just as God has a kingdom agenda that involves His comprehensive rule over every area of life, Satan has an agenda as well.[1] Satan uses deception in order to accomplish his agenda of bringing the world under his influence and control. He also seeks to make Christians ineffective in the spiritual battles waging all around us, thus reducing the glory believers give to God. Satan pursues his agenda by intentionally penetrating the same four realms that God works through to manifest His glory: the individual, family, church, and society.

---

[1] See my book *The Kingdom Agenda* (Chicago: Moody, 2006) for a complete discussion on this subject.

The Individual

Scripture makes it clear whom Satan is targeting in his schemes. First Peter 5:8 tells us, "Be of sober spirit, be on the alert. Your adversary, the devil, prowls around like a roaring lion, seeking someone to devour." To put it another way: Satan is after *you*. No matter who you are, what your status is, what your income is, how successful you are, or how well known you happen to be, Satan seeks to overpower you. What's worse is that he has become very successful at carrying out his schemes in an effort to do just that.

In fact, if we look closely enough in Christian circles today, we will find many brothers and sisters who are POWs in camps run by demons. Satan has overpowered them in the areas of drugs, alcohol, relationships, sex, bitterness, hopelessness, discouragement, low self-esteem, depression, arrogance, and codependency. Psychologists have fancy names for all of these and more, but essentially what Satan has done is turned an overcoming, blood-bought child of the King into a POW held hostage to mental instabilities and inaccuracies. If Satan can cripple or destroy an individual, he is that much further along in crippling families, churches, and societies.

The Family

The second realm that Satan seeks to penetrate is the family. We saw this initially when Satan tempted Eve and

Eve then tempted Adam, thus bringing the entire family under the authority of hell. We also saw it when demonized men had relationships with the women on earth, producing a generation of rebels (see Genesis 6). There have been countless ways that Satan attacked the family in the Bible and over the course of history.

Why is the family so important to Satan? Because in Genesis 3:15 we learn that God will use the seed of mankind to bruise Satan in battle. The spiritual battle will be waged by the offspring. This is one reason God has issued the command in Genesis 1:28 to Christians to "be fruitful and multiply, and fill the earth, and subdue it."

Satan wants to destroy you as an individual, but he wants to destroy your family even more. If he can destroy your family, he can do more damage than simply destroying the present generation. By destroying your family, he increases the potential to destroy future generations. This is because if he can get to your children before you have a chance to mold, shape, direct, and guide them correctly, he not only has influence over your home but also has influence over their future homes. If they are given over to strongholds in their lives, they will be less equipped to raise their children in such a way that will teach them to live in obedience to Christ. If their children cannot raise their own children according to God's principles, then those children will also be ill-equipped to raise their children well. A cycle will repeat itself down through several generations.

The tragedy today is that many Christians think they are fighting flesh and blood in their marital and parenting issues, rather than realizing that Satan has an agenda to destroy their home. Whoever controls the family controls the future.

The Church

The third realm Satan attacks is the church. He does this by manipulating and exploiting personality weaknesses and preferences in order to promote division, denominationalism, legalism, and other things. Satan wants to split the family of God because he understands something that many Christians do not: God's work and involvement is greatly reduced in a context of disunity. There must be harmony brought about through a genuine and authentic humility and a biblically defined love in order to witness the fullest manifestation of God's presence and power.

If Satan can divide the body of Christ along class, racial, gender, and personality lines, he can deceive entire churches into making governmental and functioning decisions based on personal partiality rather than on God's viewpoint.

Fellowship in the body of Christ is based on our allegiance to Christ. He is our standard. We may have different preferences of music, worship, or teaching, or we may even have idiosyncratic differences between various

branches of the faith, but our one unifying factor is Jesus
Christ—His death, burial, and resurrection. This is why
God tells us in Ephesians 4:3 that we are to "preserve the
unity" within the body of Christ. Satan seeks to divide us
because in doing so he lessens our effect in advancing the
kingdom of God.[2]

The Society

The fourth realm Satan targets is the society. In Dan-
iel chapter 10, we see how Satan is behind the rulers of
nations. He is behind the Hitlers, Mussolinis, Idi Amins,
and countless other rulers who have wrought havoc on
innocent people around them. Satan frequently strives
to provoke, empower, and enable them to destroy entire
nations and groups of people.

When sin entered the world, it corrupted not only
individuals but also human institutions that comprise
societies as well. Satan seeks to capitalize on this corrup-
tion to such a degree as to make societies into entities that
oppress personal freedom and opportunity rather than
serve as instruments, as they have been designed by God,
to promote biblical justice. The Bible is clear that God
has made distinct arrangements, or covenants, through
which He works. He works with the individual, family,

---

[2] For more in-depth teaching on the issue of unity and the kingdom, see
   my book *Oneness Embraced* (Chicago: Moody, 2011).

church, and government. All have been created by God and are to be influenced by God.

When you understand Satan's agenda to overpower individuals, families, churches, and ultimately societies as a whole, you can understand the complex nature of the spiritual battle we're in. Until we trace the origin of personal POW status, family POW status, church POW status, and societal POW status, Satan has us defeated in the body of Christ because he has us wrestling against flesh and blood rather than against principalities, powers, and world forces located in the heavenly places.

Satan's Strategy

Just like any excellent military commander or athletic coach, Satan has a strategy—a game plan—for accomplishing his agenda. His strategy has many parts, and before we dig deeper into what we need to do to suit up for battle, I want to look at Satan's strategic approach.

One of the devil's main tricks is to cause you to miss the goodness of God. As he did with Eve in the garden, Satan wants to get you to question the value of all of the trees that God has provided by getting you to focus on the one tree He has said to avoid. Satan wants you to complain about what you don't have so you will lose sight of what God has given you. However, God instructs us how to counteract this scheme in Philippians 4:6-8.

Be anxious for nothing, but in everything by prayer and supplication *with thanksgiving* let your requests be made known to God. And the peace of God, which surpasses all comprehension, will guard your hearts and your minds in Christ Jesus.

Finally, brethren, whatever is true, whatever is honorable, whatever is right, whatever is pure, whatever is lovely, whatever is of good repute, if there is any excellence and if anything worthy of praise, dwell on these things.

God tells us to start by praising and thanking Him for all the things He has provided. He wants us to begin by giving thanks for all He has done and by thinking about His goodness—not only in our own lives but also in the world around us.

Satan tries to pull our focus away from the goodness of God because he knows that the only way he can defeat us is through deception. Truth exists within the goodness of God, and wherever the truth of God is present, Satan's ability to deceive is diminished.

Keep in mind as you face Satan's tricks of deception that you cannot fight him on your own, with your own methods, or even with your own thoughts. God's Word—His truth—trumps Satan. *You don't.* Satan has constitutional superiority over every man and woman because he is a spirit being. He is not bound by the limitations of flesh and blood. Therefore, you cannot compete with him on the level of his deception. He is the master chameleon.

In fact, Satan is such a masterful chameleon that rarely will you find him strutting his stuff in a red jumpsuit carrying a pitchfork. That's too obvious. His scheme is to trick you. He doesn't want you to see him for who he truly is. He's not merely hanging out at the First Church of Satan. Rather, he's also concerned with finding a way to infiltrate First Baptist, First Methodist, or First Bible Church of Anytown, USA.

Not long ago, I sat down after a long day to spend some time relaxing in front of the television. A popular old show called *The Outer Limits* was playing on one of the stations. I had seen this show before, but this time something stood out. There was a clear similarity between what was playing on the television and what Satan often does in our own lives.

The Cliff Notes version of this show is that a ship had crashed in an alien environment. One of the human prisoners was taken captive and fiercely interrogated. When he wouldn't give up any information, the aliens tried another approach. They sent a beautiful young woman into the room with him to be incarcerated as a prisoner as well. As the two prisoners talked and as days drifted into weeks, they shared secrets with each other.

Over a period of time, scales began to appear on the woman after she would be taken away for questioning and then returned to the cell. The man was concerned for her and asked her what they were doing to her when they took her. She told him that they were injecting her with something that was turning her into them.

Eventually, she became completely scaled and looked like the alien creatures questioning her every day. It was at this point that they came to take her away for good. But this was only after she had successfully retrieved all of the information that there was to get out of the man. As she was leaving, the man said, "You have completely changed."

She stopped, turned around to face him, and replied, "No, I have completely changed *back*. I was always this way. I was just made to look like you so I could get your information. Now that I've got it, I can go back to being who I really am."

The devil is no different. He comes to us as an angel of light in forms we rarely recognize because he wants to steal from each of us what God has in store for us. However, once he achieves his goal, we end up seeing him for who he truly is.

Four Stages in the Strategy

Desire

There are four stages in Satan's strategy of spiritual warfare. The first stage begins with desire. A common term we often associate with desire is the word "lust." Lust is not necessarily a bad word, nor is desire a negative thing to have. Legitimate desire motivates us in our lives and provides an avenue for obtaining satisfaction and delight. However, when desire or lust manifests itself through illegitimate means, it turns into temptation, giving the potential for sin.

Desire for food is good; gluttony is a sin. Desire for sex is good; immorality is a sin. Desire for sleep is good; laziness is a sin. Satan's initial strategic point in our lives is to play on a legitimate God-given desire within us and twist it into something illegitimate. He knows the desire cannot be avoided or ignored—God has planted it within us. So Satan tries to warp that desire by influencing how it is directed and used. Essentially, he wants the desire to be the master over you rather than you being the master over your desire.

Deception

The second stage in Satan's strategy is the use of deception. A great illustration of this is how a fisherman sets out to catch a fish. If a fisherman were to put a hook into the water all by itself, he would be waiting a long time before anything ever took a bite. In fact, it's doubtful that anything would ever bite his hook. Instead, what the fisherman does is put a worm on the hook to deceive the fish into thinking it's getting a tasty meal.

Satan doesn't simply throw unbaited hooks out to us either. He doesn't advertise the local tavern by saying, "Come here and get drunk, become addicted to drugs or alcohol, lose your family, lead your kids into alcoholism, and throw away your future." Rather, what Satan does can be called the "foot in the door" technique. This was a common technique for traveling salesmen. They understood that if they could get potential customers to allow them to put their foot inside the door and talk about something unrelated to the sale, they would more than likely also have the sale. To do this, they diverted the potential customer's attention to something else.

Satan tries to get believers to let him into their lives little by little just like that. First, it's just a foot in the door—maybe a movie you shouldn't have watched, a conversation you shouldn't have had, or a relationship that shouldn't have been redefined in such a way. At first, it seemed harmless. But as Satan makes his way in, it becomes easier to graduate to the next level and buy what he is selling.

The primary way Satan does this is by planting an illegitimate or sinful idea in our minds, just as he did with David: "Then Satan stood up against Israel and *moved* David to number Israel" (1 Chronicles 21:1). David got the idea that he didn't need God at that point and that he was able to take care of his army himself. As a result, he disobeyed God's instructions, and 70,000 people ended up losing their lives. Whatever controls our minds controls our actions.

Disobedience

The third stage in Satan's strategy is disobedience. Desire leads to deception, which then leads to disobedience. The first half of James 1:15 tells us, "When lust has conceived, it gives birth to sin." Desire is not sin. Sin is the illegitimate application and placement of desire. For example, when a young child makes a decision, it's often based on feelings and desires. The child feels like playing, watching TV, eating, running, or anything of that sort. The child says, "I want that" or "I don't want that." If the desire is not managed, it can end up dominating the child's actions in forms of disobedience. However, as the child matures into adulthood, the process of maturity leads him or her to begin to operate based on the will. He or she may not feel like getting up and going to work, but because it is a responsibility, he or she gets up and goes to work.

Victorious Christian living occurs when the Holy Spirit's presence is free to manage—through our spirit—our feelings, emotions, and desires. That's not to say we need to negate our feelings. We are human beings, and emotions are very real. But the placement of their expression must be brought underneath the Spirit's control, or we run the risk of letting our volatile emotions be used by Satan to lead us straight into sin.

Philippians 2:13 says, "It is God who is at work in you, both to will and to work for His good pleasure." Victory in spiritual warfare involves intimacy and identification with Jesus Christ to such a degree that His will reveals itself as the dominant force in our own will. That is the difference between victory and defeat. Only when God's will directs our lives are we then also equipped with the power to do what He wills us to do. God promises to give us this power if and when our will aligns with His. But to do this requires faith that God knows what He is talking about. The opposite of faith is not doubt. The opposite of faith is disobedience.

Death

Satan's intention in spiritual warfare is to cause us to miss out on the goodness of God, leading us onto a path of destruction. We learned from James 1:15 that lust gives birth to sin. Here's the second half of that verse: "And when sin is accomplished, it brings forth death." Sin produces death in a variety of ways, all of which diminish our ability to experience God's promise of the abundant life. This death can show up as the death of a dream, relationship, career, virtue, or any number of other things. Primarily, sin produces a death within the fullness of our spirits as our fellowship is broken with God.

Breaking fellowship with God makes us ineffective as believers who have been designed to experience God and to glorify Him in all we do. As we saw earlier, Satan's goal is to make us ineffective. He does this through a strategy of taking a legitimate desire and guiding it down a path toward sin. Oftentimes, the death in our relationships, hopes, careers, families, or in other areas will lead to depressing thoughts and discouragement. Depression and discouragement are Satan's aim because he seeks to make our lives void of the abundance Jesus has promised us. As a result, we often question God and His promises. Not only that, but when our lives feel miserable, we are frequently too dejected to give God any glory or to tell others about Him. In fact, many of us even end up blaming God for the misery we're experiencing.

In time, Satan tries to work himself out of a job by training the deceived to become deceivers themselves (see 2 Timothy 3:13). He turns people into "evangelists of deception" who quickly and effectively spread his lies among us.

Because Satan does not have the power of creation, he has to maximize the potential of deception. He has turned deception into an art form. In fact, his skill at deceiving mankind will one day be so powerful that his antichrist will sit in the temple as god, and people will truly believe that he *is* god.

Yielding to Hell

Satan's agenda and his strategy are all-encompassing,

but there's something you and I need to know about both: *They have already been defeated.* In fact, Satan and his minions have already lost this battle. Any advancement they make in your life or on this earth is because they have been given permission to do so. The only power they have is the power that is granted to them. Satan was able to get access to ruling planet Earth only because Adam and Eve gave him permission to do it. Essentially, demons need permission from us to bring hell to us.

If hell is happening in your life, it is because hell has been given permission to do so. Hell was told—either through sin or circumstance—that you were willing to yield. You communicated something like this:

- "Hell, it's okay for you to rule my mind. It's okay for you to rule my emotions. It's okay for you to rule my will or my body."

- "I give you permission to tell me that I'm not really a man even though I was born a male."

- "I give you permission to tell me I'm not really a woman even though I was born a female."

- "I give you permission to tell me that I want drugs, I need drugs, and I can't stop using drugs."

- "I give you permission to tell me I need a

drink, can't live without a drink, and can't go
to sleep without a drink."

- "I give you permission to tell me that I
  should wake up depressed, stay depressed,
  and go to bed depressed."

- "I give you permission to tell me that I can't
  control my anger, my spending, or my
  desires; that I am not loved or that I will
  never amount to anything of significance."

The list of things we allow Satan to tell us can go on
forever. Some of it may certainly be related to chemicals
or biological malfunctions, but much of what we even
call "mental illness" today is actually caused by demons
who have been given permission to make someone men-
tally unstable.

After more than 35 years of working with individuals
through struggles in their lives as a pastor and counselor,
I'm convinced that much of what we label or try to drug
away is simply a result of Satan having his way. I'm not
saying that the physical components aren't real, but they
are often incited and encouraged by demons who have
been allowed to roam free.

Satan operates by consent and cooperation. He
operates by subtly changing the worldview, beliefs, and
thought patterns of the individual, family, church, or

society that he's targeting. Once those schemes are adopted, he is given greater permission to make himself at home. Much like roaches that have been allowed to stay in a filthy kitchen, demons that have set up camp are difficult to drive off.

I've often heard it said that some people are just too demon conscious. Maybe you feel that way. Perhaps this is the first book you've picked up on spiritual warfare because you think people sometimes make too big a deal about demons and the spiritual realm. But that's exactly what Satan would like you to believe. As long as he can keep your focus on the physical manifestations instead of the spiritual root, you will forever be fighting the wrong battle. It's hard to win a war when you don't even know where to show up to do battle.

The foundational principle for a life of total victory is this: *We do not wrestle against flesh and blood.* When we think people are our problem, we will continually be addressing people and miss the root of the problem altogether. If one of us were to set our minds on the spiritual world and less on other people, more of us might still be in our right minds. But when people's minds are divided—fighting this person, that challenge, or some other issue—they don't seem to have much of a mind left at all.

The people are real. The problems are real. The health issues are real. The challenges are real. The conflicts are real. The strongholds are real. They are just not the root of the problem.

The job of Satan and his demons is to keep you and me from experiencing the abundant life God has in store for us, and they do that by distracting us from focusing on the root. Doing that is their full-time occupation. And we are not their first job assignment. They have had plenty of years to study, practice, and perfect what they do.

But God, who is not bound by time or space, has already won this battle. Learning His strategy is our key to overcoming Satan and his demons and living a life of victory.

3

THE STRATEGY
FOR THE BATTLE

A father and his son were traveling across the Wild West in a wagon one day when a prairie fire broke out. The father and his son tried to outrun the wildfire in their wagon, but they quickly realized that it wasn't going to work. The fire was coming too fast, and unless they tried something else, it would catch up to them and consume them.

Much to the confusion of the son, the father turned the horse and wagon around and rushed directly back toward the fire. He took them to a spot that had already been burned and yelled to his son, "Jump out and stand here. Don't move!"

They both jumped out, but the boy became afraid as he saw the fire raging and moving toward them. He wanted to run, but his father grabbed his hand and said, "Don't move, son. Stand firm!"

"But the fire is almost here," the son cried, his voice shaking with fear. "I don't understand!"

"This spot has already been burned," his dad replied. "There is nothing left for the fire to grab. The fire will come near, but it cannot burn again what has already been burned once before." The boy was safe because he stayed with his father in a place that the fire could not reach.

As Satan battles you in spiritual warfare, he wants you to step away from the ground that has already been burned in the spiritual realm, which is Jesus Christ. Jesus has already been crucified, and His resurrection has already secured the victory. Satan can't touch you when you stay close to Christ. If you stand firm in the center of the safest location—the cross, where the victory has been accomplished—you will stand victoriously because Satan can't reach you there.

But that raises a question. How do you stand firm? As Paul said in Ephesians 6:10, we are to "be strong in the Lord and in the strength of His might." You stand firm by appropriating God's strength, not your own determination, positive thinking, or even self-discipline. While those things are good, they are not good enough to overcome an enemy battling you from another realm. Instead, you are to be *strong in the Lord Jesus Christ and in His might*.

In order to know how to be strong in Jesus Christ, we need to understand a few things about His power and His authority to exercise that power. For us to fully experience the power of Christ, we need to look at how things began.

When God created man, He made a very significant decision. He created Adam out of the dust of the ground, and then He said, "Let them rule" (Genesis 1:26). By letting mankind rule on earth, God willingly imposed a limitation on His own involvement in human affairs. He erected precise boundaries where He would respond, either for good or for bad, based on the decisions of men.

It was up to Adam, therefore, to use his God-given capacity to cultivate and rule his world. But in order to do that, Adam had to withstand the attacks of a sly serpent in the garden.

The problem was that Adam *did not* withstand the deceptive attack of the serpent. In fact, he allowed that serpent a strong presence in the garden, forcing Adam out. As a result, Adam allowed the serpent to rule in his place. In football language, we would say Adam fumbled the ball in the devil's red zone, and the serpent recovered it.

What caused the fumble? Eve had gotten out of alignment under Adam, and Adam had gotten out of alignment under God. This stripped the ball called "rule" from Adam's hands and gave it to Satan. He took possession of the garden from that point on.

So cataclysmic was Adam's fumble that Satan and his team sprinted down the field all of the way to mankind's red zone. Now they have the ball, they call the plays, and they are running out the clock. Because of the fumble, the Adamites—the human race—have been scrambling ever since.

And that's what we're doing, even to this day. I hear it all of the time. Maybe you hear it too. People talk about trying to stop the devil. If you are trying to stop the devil, he's obviously coming after you. He has the ball. He's calling the shots. He's running the show. He's setting the agenda. And the reason you're trying to stop him is that you are now in a defensive mode.

Jesus recognized this change of position by referring to Satan three times as the ruler of this world (John 12:31; 14:30; 16:11). Because of Adam's fumble, Satan is the one who now calls the plays in this world. Of course Satan can only govern the world within the sovereign boundaries set up by God, the ultimate Governor, but he still rules through deception, intimidation, and a myriad of other means.

Not only that, but when Satan took over the rule of this world, a curse came with it. This curse affected Adam's career, family, finances, children, security, and even his life. And unless you and I understand the theology of authority, we will never overcome the curse handed off to us by Adam, and we will never be completely victorious in spiritual warfare.

The bad news is that Satan recovered Adam's fumble. The good news is that you can get the ball back. You can live in both hope and victory when you stand firm in the strength of Christ. You can force another fumble—this time, by Satan—and in so doing recover the authority that has already been secured for you.

If you have come to Jesus Christ for the forgiveness of your sins and for the gift of eternal life that He freely offers, you have already forced that fumble. Now all you need to do is pick up the ball and run with it. Through Christ's sacrificial atonement, you have already been repositioned for victory in your life. Remember, you are not fighting *for* victory—you are fighting *from* victory. Let's find out how.

Headship and Authority

When God pronounced the curse to the serpent for luring Adam out from underneath his designated alignment, He coupled it with a prophecy: "I will put enmity between you and the woman, and between your seed and her seed; He shall bruise you on the head, and you shall bruise him on the heel" (Genesis 3:15).

In these words, God said, "Adam, you have fumbled the ball. You have turned over the rule of your life, and others' lives, to the evil one by moving out from underneath My alignment. Adam, you blew it—big-time. But I've got some good news for you because a woman is going to have a child. And that child will have His heel hurt by the serpent, but that same child—the seed of the woman—will crush the serpent's head."

He will crush the serpent's head. Don't read that too quickly. God said that the seed of the woman will crush the serpent's head. Let me help you grasp the significance of that statement by adding something onto the end of a word. Look at it this way:

The seed of the woman will crush the serpent's head*ship*.

"Headship" means rule and authority. With the coming of the seed of the woman—Jesus Christ—the headship (the rule and authority of Satan) has been crushed. Eliminated. *Gone!* The heel of the seed was wounded in the process, along with His humanity, on the cross, but when all was said and done, Satan's headship was crushed, and Jesus Christ negated the devil's authoritative rule.

That truth alone is enough for you to know that you can get back on the offense in this life. On the cross and through the resurrection, Jesus Christ has already crushed Satan's authority. It's a done deal. The whistle has blown. The play is dead. The ball is now yours once again. In fact, when Jesus spoke about His future death on the cross, He declared Satan's ultimate removal of authority: "Now judgment is upon this world; now the ruler of this world will be cast out. And I, if I am lifted up from the earth, will draw all men to Myself" (John 12:31-32).

This is so vitally important that I want to put it another way just to make sure we're on the same page. *When you come to Jesus Christ and accept His sacrifice for your life, you are putting yourself under the new Head of State.* The head of state is the one who has final authority for the matters in that land. In America, the head of state is our president. Our president, by virtue of his office, holds the final and ultimate say on what goes on in our nation. It is what we call "veto power."

When the opposition to the president passes a law that he does not approve of, he doesn't have to accept it. He can disarm it with his veto power. With one stroke of his pen, he can literally undo what took hours, days, and even months for Congress to enact.

Jesus Christ, through the power of the cross and resurrection, has the ultimate veto power in our world. Satan no longer holds final authority over your life. Sure, he may spend hours, days, months, years, and even decades persuading you to believe his lies and pressuring you into feeling that he has the final authority over you, but once you realize that Jesus Christ has already defeated him, you will be set free to live your life in victory. Satan got pummeled at Calvary. He dropped the ball. He knows that. God knows that too.

The problems come, though, when *we* don't know that truth and stand firm in it. Knowledge—what you know and what you believe about a matter—is vital. It's one thing for someone to point a gun at you that has bullets in it. But it's entirely something else for someone to point a gun at you that is empty. Both people do not have the same power over you. One of them has been disarmed. His firepower has been removed.

It's just that we don't always know that. We don't always have adequate knowledge for a situation like that. If a gun were pointed at us, we wouldn't have any way of knowing whether it was loaded. To be safe, most likely we would walk, talk, and act as if the gun is loaded.

But let me ask you something: What would you do if somebody let you know that the gun was empty? Or what if you saw the gun fired six times, and all six times, nothing came out? What then? Would you still be making your decisions based on that gun? Probably not. And neither would I because that empty gun no longer holds any authority. We have no need to fear an empty gun.

Of course, the devil doesn't want us to know that his gun has been emptied at the cross of Jesus Christ. So he keeps pointing it at us and putting it in our face as if it were loaded. And we don't realize it's empty, so we keep bowing under its presence. We don't realize that at the cross, Jesus Christ took the bullets out of Satan's gun. We don't realize that the most the devil can do is pretend that his gun is still loaded.

If you don't know that Satan's guns are not loaded, you're going to act as if you're defeated because you will erroneously believe he has power over you.

And that's how many of us live our lives. We forget

that at the cross, Jesus Christ deactivated, dismantled, and disarmed Satan's headship.

Satan has lost his authority. Or, to make it more personal: Satan no longer has any authority over *you*.

Authority Versus Power

"Hey that's nice, Tony," you say. "It sounds very heavenly minded and ethereal, and it even looks good on paper. But what about me living down here in the real world with real battles—financial wars, career wars, family wars, and emotional wars? What about those? I don't seem to be living in victory in my wars. Rather, my enemies are being victorious over me. Yet you're telling me that Jesus Christ is the head. You're telling me that Jesus Christ is calling the plays now and that I'm underneath His authority. So what gives? That's not what's going on in my life."

Those are good questions that we all face. To answer them, we need to keep in mind this essential truth: *Satan lost his authority, but he didn't lose his power.* Satan still dominates our world in many ways because he has retained his power. Satan is as powerful now as he has ever been. The things he does are real, damaging, and destructive. He is and will always be a liar, thief, and murderer with intentions to kill, steal, and destroy. It only takes a glance around our globe, around our communities and homes, or even in our own souls to see that Satan still operates with power.

The truth we need to realize, and the truth that will set us free, is that Satan no longer has authority. That is the key.

Authority is the right to use the power that you possess.

In order for Satan to use his power in your life, he now has to keep you from functioning underneath your authority because his power is only effective when he has the right to use it. Satan does not have the authority to use his power when you are living underneath your legitimate authority as a Christian. Therefore, he seeks to lure you out from underneath God's authority and rule in your life because he knows that you are secure underneath Him. Colossians 1:13 tells us that God has "rescued us from the domain of darkness, and transferred us to the kingdom of His beloved Son." God rescued us out of the wrong kingdom and brought us into the right one. By rescuing us, He brought us under the rule of a new King. You used to be under Satan's rule before you met Christ, but now you are part of a new kingdom of which Jesus Christ is the King. Satan, in order to rule your world, must entice you to leave your kingdom and come back over to his.

The reason we don't experience more victory in spiritual warfare is that we've been duped into believing that attending church on Sunday and simply getting more information about the real kingdom is enough. Or maybe we think that adding a Wednesday night Bible study will be sufficient to affirm our allegiance to our King. Or maybe we'll toss in some serving and praise songs and think we've got it covered.

But then we go back to work on Monday, or back to our routine at home with our mate or with our children, and we flip back over into our old way of thinking. We slide back into the other kingdom and operate under its authority. We align our thoughts with the wisdom Satan has set up in this world. We base our decisions on how we feel or what our friends are telling us or even what our fears are telling us. We transfer our allegiance from the conclusive and authoritative Word of God through Jesus Christ back to Satan's worldly schemes.

We wind up not being victorious in spiritual warfare because we keep flipping sides. We come to church under one kingdom, but we operate on the job in another kingdom. We have our devotions in one kingdom, but we operate among our friends in another kingdom. We keep flip-flopping kingdoms and wonder why the victory is not there. We wonder why we can't get over the hump. We wonder why the enemy keeps calling the plays. We wonder why our prayers go unanswered, our battles end in defeat, and our power over our own lives runs out. The opposition keeps intercepting the ball and returning it for a touchdown.

But the answer is simple: The enemy is victorious in our lives because we are yielding the power to him by not standing firm in our identity in Jesus Christ. We are failing to firmly remain in the union we were designed to have with Christ, under His headship.

Our Union with Christ

Our union with Christ is essential to our victory over Satan's rule in our lives. The book of Colossians goes into great detail about this.

> See to it that no one takes you captive through hollow and deceptive philosophy, which depends on human tradition and the basic principles of this world rather than on Christ. For in Christ all the fullness of the Deity lives in bodily form, and *you have been given fullness in Christ, who is the head over every power and authority.* In him you were also circumcised, in the putting off of the sinful nature, not with a circumcision done by the hands of men but with the circumcision done by Christ, having been buried with him in baptism and raised with him through your faith in the power of God, who raised him from the dead (Colossians 2:8-12 NIV).

Everything that makes up God—His essence and totality—is in Christ, fully. The only difference is that it's in a human body. "For in Christ *all* the fullness of the Deity lives in bodily form."

All of the fullness of God is in Jesus Christ. Not some, not a bit, but *all*.

That's why Jesus is the Son of Man *and* the Son of God. That's why He can get thirsty one minute, and the next minute He can go out and walk on water. That's why He can get hungry one day, and the next day He turns sardines and crackers into a Moby Dick sandwich to feed more than 5000 people. That's why Jesus can die—and then *get up*! He can do all of these things because He is the God-man; fully God and fully man in one person. "For *in* Christ all the fullness of the Deity lives in bodily form."

In fact, if we were to backtrack a few paragraphs, we discover even more.

> He [Jesus] is the image of the invisible God, the firstborn over all creation. For by him all things were created: things in heaven and on earth, visible and invisible, whether thrones or powers or rulers or authorities; all things were created by him and for him. He is before all things, and in him all things hold together (Colossians 1:15-17 NIV).

Jesus Christ holds all things together. Therefore, if you find yourself falling apart, it is a result of you not having stood firm with Jesus in union with Him. We are told that *in* Him, all things hold together and maintain their equilibrium. Take a look at these very important phrases in Colossians 2:

- "in Him" (verse 9)
- "in Him" (verse 10)
- "in Him" (verse 11)
- "with Him…with Him" (verse 12)
- "with Him" (verse 13)

Do you see the pattern? Our victory in spiritual warfare is intimately connected to Jesus Christ. *In* Him. *With* Him. If we miss this truth, we miss the key to our victory: our union with Jesus Christ. Let me illustrate a little bit about that union.

Our church in Oak Cliff becomes a vibrant place of worship, fellowship, outreach, and teaching each and every Sunday morning for thousands of people. If you ever find yourself in the Dallas area on a Sunday, I invite you to come. I would love to meet you personally and let you experience the unique atmosphere in the sanctuary we call Oak Cliff Bible Fellowship. Sundays are a highlight of my week. I enjoy gathering with the saints.

But by Sunday afternoon, I admit, after having sung, sat, and preached through two two-hour-long services, I'm tired.

Knowing this is going to happen, I usually start my Sunday morning with a cup of coffee. Now, some people like their coffee black, and that's fine if that's how you like your coffee. But I always like to have some cream in my coffee.

So every Sunday, before I drink my coffee, I get the white cream and pour it into my black coffee. Then I take the stick and stir it so that a *union* occurs between my black coffee and my white cream. When that happens, there is no longer any black coffee or white cream. Instead, I now have brown coffee. It is brown because a union has occurred.

If I want to take my formerly black coffee with me into my office before the service, the cream must come along as well. If I want to take my cream into the prayer room, my once-black coffee will be coming with it as well. Once they are mixed, wherever one goes, the other must go as well simply by virtue of the union that has occurred.

This is how our relationship with Christ has been designed, as we saw earlier in Ephesians: "Even when we were dead in our transgressions, [God] made us alive *together* with Christ (by grace you have been saved), and raised us up *with* Him, and seated us *with* Him in the heavenly places *in* Christ Jesus" (Ephesians 2:5-6).

When Christ died, we died with Him. When Christ arose, we arose with Him. When Christ was seated at the right hand of the Father, we were seated with Him. In other words, we were made to function in union with Christ.

Jesus Christ *is* over all things; He is sovereign over everything. He has recovered the fumbled ball and has legal authority and victory in the spiritual realm. For us to access that victory, we must stand firm under His headship in our thoughts, in our actions, in our hearts, in our decisions, on our job, in our homes, and throughout our lives.

Only when we stand firm under His Word and authority will we be able to live victoriously in spiritual warfare. Friend, you can go to all of the meetings you want. You can read all of the self-help books and magazines you want. You can name and claim whatever you want. But until you stand firm under the comprehensive rule of God in your life and in union with your identity in Jesus Christ, you will only find a temporary reprieve. Only in Christ will you find the authority to live in victory.

I often hear people quoting the Scripture, "If the Son makes you free, you will be free indeed." But when I look around me, I see very few people who are free *indeed*. And the reason is that we have settled for the temporary rather than aligning ourselves with eternity. Satan has already been beaten. He has already been disarmed. The bullets have already been removed. The fumble has already been recovered. Jesus has already defeated Satan. He is already victorious. And you are in union with Him.

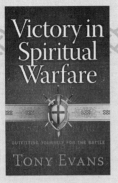

For more biblical insights on how you can win your own spiritual battles, you can read Tony Evans' powerful book, *Victory in Spiritual Warfare.*

Dr. Evans has also created a book of prayers that you can use to win the fight against Satan in *Prayers for Victory in Spiritual Warfare.*

Both resources are available from your favorite bookseller.